Bridging Troubled Waters

The Memoirs of
Voni B. Grimes

To:

Matthew, my friend,

Love,

Voni B. Grimes

2009.

I DEDICATE THIS BOOK TO
MY MOTHER

MITTIE G. GRIMES

HER SONG:
"I'M GOING TO LET MY LITTLE LIGHT SHINE"

SUN UP:	SUN DOWN:
APRIL 20, 1892	FEBRUARY 3, 1986

Foreword
By James McClure

Voni B. Grimes was born three years before investors launched The Yorktowne Hotel toward its 11-story height.

As a youngster growing up around York, Grimes viewed the hotel as a towering symbol of achievement, the place to stay in York County.

He still does, and it still is.

But Grimes was aware that touring black performers could not lodge there. They often ended up at Helen Peaco's place on Cleveland Avenue.

And he couldn't land a job there, although the hotel employed blacks as bellmen, cooks and elevator operators.

He figured his work application was rejected because "Mr. Russell," who hired waiters, believed he had the potential for higher education. He couldn't really move up at the Yorktowne. No blacks could in those days.

The tall building represented a mammoth obstacle for black people to surmount.

But he would stay at the Yorktowne.

"I'm going to live there someday," he vowed.

Somehow.

* * *

Voni Grimes was searching for help in writing his memoirs. Some people had asked him to put into writing his 80-plus years of achievement.

Others could learn from his successes, they told him. Indeed, he is filling a line of big footsteps led by the late Dr. George Bowles, the Rev. Thomas E. Montouth and W. Russell Chapman as senior statesmen in the black community.

Grimes had arrived at the crossroads that many reach when encouraged to write about their lives.

Should I write my autobiography?

Some do. Most don't.

But how to do it?

Grimes asked the same question.

Just tell your story, I replied. Start at the beginning, in Bamberg, S.C., and work to the present day.

I wrote on a sheet of paper what I knew of his story:

Born in the Bamberg. Came North when he was 4. Grew up in York. Served in World War II. Gained success at Cole Steel and Penn State York. Retired to a life of volunteerism, including Lions district governor.

Then his music. What's next in his life?

And we talked about how his Christian faith would overlay all these steps. And there was that wonderful goal of living in the Yorktowne that would help tie together his early and mature years.

Voni Grimes, always quick with a smile, brightened even more.

It wouldn't be easy, but he had the key.

He would just tell his story.

A month later, he was doing just that. He wrote in longhand and then typed that draft into a computer.

Before long, he hit a block. His computer had run out of space.

He would need help to retrieve his work.

Writing memoirs is difficult enough, but then come computer problems.

Would he persist?

This book indicates that he did.

Talk to Voni Grimes long enough, and the Yorktowne emerges as a meaningful part of his life's story.

Written into his memoirs, it also helps his work connect with the story of York, a meta-narrative or story on top of a story.

That larger story shows York and its trademark Yorktowne changing, changing for the better.

Yorktowne officials have sensed what the hotel means to the community.

"It is the center, the soul, and the symbol of the community that built it 70 years ago," a history published in 1995 states.

The dark side of that soul formerly rejected blacks as guests. Its enlightened side now welcomes them.

Voni Grimes has seen both sides.

Over the course of his postwar life, Grimes invested in rental properties around York.

He had a plan. When he reached 50, he would start divesting of most of them.

But the plan had another part. He would live in the Yorktowne when he reached 75 years old.

At that milestone, he approached Yorktowne's management about renting there.

The hotel management ushered in Voni and his wife, Lorrayne, through their trademark revolving door.

Voni Grimes had climbed the mountain and settled near its top.

The story doesn't stop there.

After five years of living his dream in a sixth-floor suite, the press of recreational space for their grandchildren and great-grandchildren caused the Grimeses to seek an apartment with play facilities in suburban York.

"OK, I've lived my dream," he told Lorrayne. "Now, it's your turn."

Yes, and now it's Voni Grimes' turn again.

Read on, as he just tells his story.

This foreword is adapted from a column in the York Sunday News, Nov. 5, 2006.

Content

'It is better to have an education and not need it than to need an education and not have it.'

Voni B. Grimes, 2008

Chapter 1

Growing up

My name is Voni B. Grimes, born Vonidoe Buster Grimes.

I was born December 23, 1922, in a very small town called, Bamberg, South Carolina, 245 Weimer Street, son of Mittie and McKinley Grimes. My father always called me Bus, and my mother always called me Buster as a nickname. My uncle was named Vonidoe, which could have been an old African name or a French name. I'm not sure.

I remember as a four-year-old child, I had a little puppy. We were inseparable. I had a little brother who was too small to play outside with me. It was just my little puppy and me. When he would run under the house, I would chase him. I had to crawl under the house after him. Then he would run from under the house, and so on. At noon, I would hear the whistle blowing from the cotton mill where my father worked. That whistle was a joy, because it told me that my father was coming home for lunch. I would run through the garden in the back yard, through the fence and through the field with my puppy following to meet my father coming home. It was important to me to hear that whistle blow, because I knew my father would be coming across the field to meet me and hold my hand as we approached the house, with my puppy bringing up the rear.

During the same year, 1926, my family decided to move to York, Pennsylvania. My uncle told my father that jobs were easy to find, and the pay was good. This meant I had to give my puppy away. After we packed our suitcases, we headed to the train station to catch a train bound for Pennsylvania. I never saw a train close-up before, so that was a new experience for me. I don't know how my little brother, in my mother's arms, responded, but I started running away. The train was huge, and the steam was rushing out from each side. My father had to catch me. I was really frightened, especially when the whistle blew. It sounded nothing like the noon whistle I was used to hearing.

When we arrived in York, my aunt and uncle met us at the station. York was much larger than Bamberg. We lived with them for a short time, then moved to the 600 block of East King Street, paying $10 a month rent. My father got a job at CertainTeed Corporation, a roofing materials manufacturer, earning 30 cents an hour or $12 a week. He bought a bicycle to ride to work across town, for it was too far to walk. However, he did walk for a week. His job was working in the rag room. Rags included old books, helmets made of material, old clothing and so on. These items came from everywhere, including from abroad. He used to bring home books written in various languages. I am 85 years old, and I still have a Chinese poetry book and pictures made of rice paper. I had a black helmet with a metal ornament on top. It could have been from Germany. He brought home clothing that he thought would fit my brother and me. My mother would wash the shirts and pants on the scrub board with 'lye soap' placed in a washtub to make them wearable. At that time, a loaf of bread was 5 cents a loaf, milk 7 cents, and meat 29 cents a pound.

My parents joined Small Memorial A. M. E. Zion Church. During that time, we moved to 527 Susquehanna Ave., four blocks east of Penn Park and five blocks east of Pershing Avenue. We had no inside plumbing or electricity in our home, nor did anyone else in that area, but we had love for others and in our home. I have been going to the A. M. E Zion Church for 80 years. However, we were not allowed to join until we were 12 years old, so I have been a member for 74 years as of 2008.

I started first grade at Smallwood School. I had to go past Noell Primary School on East College Avenue, a half block from my house, because the primary schools were segregated.

Smallwood School was five blocks west of Noell school. However, the poor whites who lived in the alley near us colored people (as we were called during that time) went to Noell school. When school was out at the end of the day, we played together, but we couldn't go to school together.

As I continued my schooling at Smallwood School and Aquilla Howard, another primary school for Negro students, I realized when we were in the fourth to sixth grades, we were given books that the white students had used. Not always. But often. Some might have been an edition they had finished, because I remembered getting a classroom book with a girl's name in it. I remember this as if it were yesterday. Mr. Hopewell, principal, asked the class to turn to page 22. That page was torn out of my book, so I told him about it. He made a joke of it, telling me to turn to page 11 two times. We all laughed. He really said that in class. He was joking. Through it all, we learned.

When I went to Hannah Penn Junior High School, it was the first time I was in class with white students. They were ahead of the Negro students in math. It wasn't that we lacked ability. We didn't have equal opportunity to achieve. In junior high, we finally were able to achieve, because we were learning out of the same books and current editions. During my stay at Hannah Penn, I had one confrontation, because a fellow student misunderstood goodness for weakness. He repeated something he must have picked up at home about colored people not being as good as whites. I just hit him. Later, we became friends, and I had no other problems.

In my years at William Penn High School, I was a good student. I studied hard. Rather than taking a study period for two semesters, I took typing. My regular classes were college preparatory: geometry, trigonometry, mechanical drawing, physics, chemistry, English and Spanish. I did well in all of those subjects. When I graduated, I received a "general" diploma, as did the other Negroes. Evidently, the thinking in local education was that we wouldn't be going to college, so it didn't make any difference. However, my dream was to go to college.

During my junior year in high school, I junked during the winter and summer. This means I went out at night when people sat their trash out, and I would take paper out of their trash and sell it. I had regular customers in the suburbs. They would save their old newspapers and clothing they thought I could use. That is what some of the young boys would do who were too young to get a job. I would also cut these customers' grass for a nickel or a dime or whatever they thought it was worth. A nickel or a dime was a lot of money at that time, because a loaf of bread was five cents for a small loaf. Everything is relative.

During the summer months when high school was out, I walked five miles, four days a week, to J. M. Miller's farm to pick strawberries, beans and gather shocks of wheat to be loaded onto hay wagons. I could earn 50 cents a day. On Saturdays, I hauled baskets for my customers at the now-demolished City Market, corner of Duke Street and College Avenue, next to a building now called the Voni B. Grimes Gym. I did the same duty at Penn Street Market, still standing at the corner of Penn and Market Streets. For those chores, I would receive a nickel or a dime, sometimes 15 cents from affluent customers. It was good money, because a large cone of ice cream was just a nickel, a loaf of bread was a nickel and a quart of milk was 12 cents. As I said before, everything is relative.

I had these jobs until I was 16 years old. Then I got a job washing dishes at the York Country Club. Eventually I was helping to make desserts. I really liked that, because it was a learning experience. I was helping to make desserts when the news came over the radio, in these pre-TV days, that the Japanese had bombed Pearl Harbor. No one really worked the rest of the day, because we did not know what was next. This was a new experience for all of us.

Although I was athletically inclined, I never played football or basketball for Hannah Penn Junior High or William Penn Senior High School. It would take too much of my time, and I was always working. However, I did manage to run track for Hannah Penn, once. Also I played table tennis for Hannah Penn, but that was all that I did. The table tennis team played other schools in York, Lancaster and Harrisburg. We learned to know other team members, and some of them became lifelong friends.

Chapter 2

Seeking higher education

When I graduated from William Penn, I immediately got a job working with the carpenters as a helper on very long warehouses at the New Cumberland Army Depot, now Defense Distribution Center in Northern York County. At that time, we were paid $36 for a 40-hour week. Bread was about 15 to 20 cents a loaf, and milk was in the same cost range. That money was very important to us because my mother was working part time at $3 a day. My mother was a staunch Christian and a supportive mother for her four children, McKinley, Erthamae, Margaret and me.

When we were very young and it was just the two of us - McKinley, Jr. (Ting, as he was called) and I - my father would put my little brother on his shoulders when he was tired of walking on our way to church. My father was a hardworking man for his family, but he was a man who loved life. My mother told me he took her to a nightclub, although she had never been in one before. After being there for a short time, she wanted to go home. My father took her home, and she told him that was not for her, but he could go back if he wanted. He liked that kind of life, so he went back that night. She told me that was the beginning of his nightlife. When I graduated from William Penn, 19M42 (mid-year), my father moved to Washington, D.C., after spending 15 years at CertainTeed Corporation. However, there was no animosity between us. We did not like his move, but we still respected each other. I had a secondhand 1938 Pontiac convertible with a rumble seat in the back, which I had paid $375 for. (I still have the form for what it cost and the monthly payments.) So my mother and her four children traveled in my car to Washington, D.C., to see my father. He told us he was working at the airport loading planes. We had a very good evening together.

In 1942, I wanted to go to Wilberforce College, but I didn't have $250 for tuition. I happened to see in the morning's paper, The Gazette and Daily (now called the York Daily Record), that there was an ad for high school graduates to apply for jobs as sheet metal workers, but most of the jobs required courses in sheet metal at the Bok Vocational School in Philadelphia. The courses were at no cost to the student, because this country was at war with Germany and Japan. It was for the war effort.

I told my mother I wanted to go to Philadelphia to sign up for that course, and she asked, "Where are you going to live?" I told her I didn't know. I had $20 in my pocket when I left York and $3.50 for my round-trip ticket, if I did not find a room near the school or at the colored Y.M.C.A. God was in the plan because I saw a man approaching me as I was walking down the street. As he neared, I asked him if he knew of anyone who rented rooms. At that time, many people rented rooms, because you could not go into many of the white hotels for lodging. He said, "I have a friend that might have a room for rent." He eagerly told me how to get there.

When I arrived at the house, there was a sign in the window at 1031 South 17th Street saying, "Room for Rent." I immediately inquired about it, and a lady answered the door. I told her about my being from York and my search for a place to stay because I had completed an application for schooling at Bok Vocational School in the sheet metal trade. She was very nice and said, "Come in, young man. What is your name?"

"My name is Voni Grimes. I'm from York, Pa.," I replied.

"That's an odd name, where did you get that name, young man?" she asked.

I told her I was named after my uncle.

"Voni, am I pronouncing it right?" she asked.

I told her yes.

She said, "My name is Mrs. Trent. My husband isn't home yet (he was an assistant coroner), but my daughter is here, and she is much older than you."

The daughter came into the room, and her mother said, "Delores, he seems like a nice young man. I'm going to rent him that extra room we have upstairs for $3 per week." Being a young Christian, I knew that God was in the plan, because He was watching over me. However, you have to know Him for yourself to reap the benefits; otherwise, you would not know He is watching over you, because I didn't know anyone in Philadelphia at that time. I rented from Mr. and Mrs. Trent for two years.

While living with the Trents, I worked at the Philadelphia Navy Yard as a sheet metal worker trainee. I studied in the day, ate lunch and dinner at Father Devine's Restaurant for 15 cents, each meal. The waitress would also pack my lunch, which would include two sandwiches, fruit and a slice of cake or pie for the same price, which I would carry to work for my 11 p.m. to 7 a.m. shift.

The sheet metal trade demands that one is knowledgeable in math and mechanical drawing. I was always good in math, and I had mechanical drawing in high school, which helped tremendously. If one wants to advance in the sheet metal industry, one has to go back to school and take more courses to become a sheet metal mechanic. I did go back to school and took the required courses and became a third-class mechanic. As a mechanic, you are given three or four helpers and a welder to tack and weld the items to be fabricated. You read your prints issued, using the proper gauge metal such as steel, aluminum and brass. The team started the job, and it was finished by the team. Everything has to be weighed. You should know how to figure it out mathematically, because each kind of metal has a different formula. The weight of a bulkhead is very unhandy, so you do it mathematically before it is formed.

During that time, there were no assembly lines in the sheet metal department. Our team consisted of two ladies and two men. Of the two ladies, I became very interested in one, and she in me. I guess that was because we both knew Jesus Christ. We would visit each other's churches. Her church was in West Philadelphia, and my church, Greater Zion, was in South Philadelphia.

Sometimes, Mr. Trent and I would just sit and talk about life in general. Especially, we discussed my job and courses in school. Hearing my stories about the job and courses, he told me how to be successful in life. He told me how he got to where he was, and how I can get to where I wanted to be. I realized as long as I had my mouth zipped, I was learning or he was confirming something I already knew. However, he said, success to you might not be success to someone else. Success to others could be a beautiful home, money or a good family. You have to decide what is successful to you in your life and work at it. He shared with me how he became successful in his own little way. However, he said he had some bad days and good days, and I would have the same. But you have to keep going until you get where you want to be.

I eventually told him about the girl I was dating. He inquired about my date, Irene Clay. I told him what he wanted to know. He said, "Good for you." However, I delayed in telling my mother. When I did tell her, she asked me to bring Irene to York for her to be introduced to the young lady. The following week, I took her to see my mother. I didn't know what she would think, because that was the first time I had introduced my mother to any girl I was dating. Up to that time, I only had girls who were friends. The three of us had a good conversation. My mother said to her, "What time are you and Voni going back to Philadelphia this evening?" I knew what that meant; take her back before night.

When I came home the following weekend, my mother said to me, "She seems like a nice young lady. Where was she born?" I said, Durham, North Carolina.

Chapter 3

Military training

I was drafted in the Army on Jan. 13, 1944, and inducted Feb. 3, 1944, in Harrisburg. I took my basic training in the Army Air Corps, Lincoln, Neb. After basic training, I was given a furlough to go home for two weeks. While home, on June 21, 1944, I took Irene Clay to be my wedded wife, a wonderful lady. She temporarily moved in with my mother and my two younger sisters, Erthamae and Margaret, after quitting her job at the Philadelphia Navy Yard as a sheet metal helper. My younger brother, McKinley, was drafted soon after his graduation, so he was not at home. My wife worked in the downtown stores in York dressing windows.

When I was transferred to Pocatello, Idaho, Air Base, I was able to continue my sheet metal trade repairing airplane wings, cowls, etc. I got permission to live off base with my wife, and she and I were very happy. We went to many activities on the base. In dance competitions, we would win a box of candy for being the best dancers. When we wanted candy, we would participate. We also had table tennis tournaments, and I would win. When I was in junior and senior high schools, I had played on the school teams. We played many schools in our district and sometimes other districts. Maybe, that was why I usually won in Army competition.

When Irene and I learned I was going to be transferred to Camp Livingston, La., she went back to York to get a job and live with my mother. She put an application in for a keypunch operator at McCrory's Distribution Center and was hired. We felt very close, because we wrote each other every day.

Later that year, I was transferred to the 92$^{nd.}$ Infantry Division (Colored), after the Battle of the Bulge, the German assault in Belgium. Eleven soldiers and I were put on a train destined for Camp Livingston. We arrived in a small town near Camp Livingston called Simms. As we got off the train, an M.P. said, "You boys get in the back and you white soldiers sit up front of this shuttle train, which will take you to the camp." The white soldiers went to their company, and we went to the 92nd. The last week of basic training was tough. We were "strafed" by low-flying planes dropping flour in the middle of the road, as we marched on both sides of the road. If any flour was on you, you were considered wounded or dead. That all happened when we were hiking 25 miles with full backpacks back to the base.

When our company was drilling in the field a week later, I received a call from the sergeant to report to the day room. As I entered, the lieutenant said, "Private Grimes, pack your duffle bag, you are shipping out."

"Where am I going, Lieutenant?" I asked.

"You are going to Fort Sill, Oklahoma. You are going to the 246th Ordnance Ammunition Company." he said.

I boarded the train for Fort Sill. Arriving there, I was met by a sergeant in a jeep. I was taken to the base to meet the lieutenant who assigned me to a barracks and told me to report to his office at 0700 the next morning. The first and second lieutenants were black, but Captain Tucker was white. There was always a higher-grade white officer. I noticed our facilities on the base were not as updated as the white soldiers'. For instance, there was a leak in the roof, and it was raining. I asked the soldier whose bunk was next to mine: Why don't they fix the leak? He said, "I told the captain, but they didn't fix it yet," so we put a bucket down to catch it. However, this could have been an isolated case of discrimination.

At Fort Sill, my spec number was 055, which was in administration personal. In high school, I had academic subjects and typing, which now qualified me for the job in the office. I became a T5, corporal. The officer in charge learned that I could type and do other duties. I kept files up to date. I used an ice pick about 24 inches long with a handle on the end to get the proper file or files out by running the pick from the front to the back of the cabinet drawer. The file folders had ears with holes in them designating the category you were seeking. I would insert the pick into the category ears, and the only thing that came up would be what I was seeking. I was also the mailman.

Chapter 4

Overseas Duty

Five or six months hence, our entire company was shipped by train to Seattle, meeting soldiers from other bases around the United States. Three thousand troops, as we were told. We were only there overnight, then we boarded a ship for somewhere. We didn't know where we were going until we had been at sea for five days. The talk was Guam, Mariana Islands. So that was why we had learned Judo for six weeks. That was just enough to get us killed. When American children are young, we purchase a ball and bat or a football. Japanese children get a judohe, which is an outfit for judo or other areas of martial arts. That is a lifetime skill we didn't have.

It took 17 days to get to Guam. We would be on deck and see the ship zigzagging. We didn't say anything, because we didn't know what to say. When we landed in Guam, we were told a Japanese sub had been following us for three days, trying to get a bead on the ship. I am glad they didn't tell us that at sea. Although we were on dry land, we were still afraid after being told.

It was raining when we disembarked, because this was the rainy season. Six by Six trucks, as they were called, were waiting to take us where we were supposed to go - not knowing we were just going to the boondocks about five miles inland instead of barracks. When the trucks stopped, we wondered why, because there wasn't anything but thickets, palm trees and bamboo.

The first sergeant said, "Dismount, all out of the trucks."

"For what?" a soldier asked harshly.

"This is where you are staying," came the reply. "You have shelter haves, so get busy and put them together and dig a trench around your pup tents so the rain water will not enter your tent."

There were many iguanas about three or four feet long everywhere in the area, although we did not know it in advance. At first, we were frightened at the sight of them. Within a week or more, the native boys who prided themselves as skilled in catching iguanas showed us how to catch them. There were Southern soldiers who saw animals all the time at home, so they learned for a reason: to further frighten those who were afraid of them. They would catch the smaller ones by the tail. Guam was an experience for all of us, seeing animals and birds that we had never seen before. Also, Guamanians - their culture, where and how they lived - fascinated us.

My job on Guam was a mailman for our company, which included censoring mail going to the United States: deleting words or sentences which would disclose information not to be given. I also did routine office work. Individual file jackets had ears with holes in certain areas indicating what was in that file by numbers. Then I used the 24-inch pick with the handle on the end – same as I had used at Fort Sill. If my captain wanted a clerk typist, I would put the pick through the ears of the files from front to back that said 055, and all 055s would be on the pick when I raised it. Then I would select as many 055s as required. That system was before keypunch, I believe, but I know it was before computers.

In July and August 1945, we were issued ammunition and everything else that was necessary for an invasion of Japan. We knew it was something that involved us, because of the attitude of our officers. We knew if we were going to invade Japan, there would be thousands and thousands of soldiers who would not make it through Tokyo Bay.

In August 1945, the atomic bomb was dropped on Hiroshima. It didn't have a crater, because it was dropped by parachute, and it exploded before it hit the ground. That was a very important Japanese city. Japanese radio said no one escaped death in its scorching path. It also said the dead were too numerous to count. Three days later, another atomic bomb was dropped on Nagasaki, wiping out 30 percent of that city. The second atomic bomb did not use a parachute, therefore creating a crater.

No country had ever used or received a bomb of that magnitude. Japan surrendered immediately, but some of the Japanese who were hiding in caves did not know Japan surrendered. The Guamanians would let us know when they saw Japanese soldiers, and we would go after them. The Army had soldiers trained for that task, but we were young, dumb and adventurous.

As five of us walked along a stream one day, we saw four Japanese soldiers about a city block away. They saw us, too. They started running. We couldn't shoot, because the war was over. As we got closer to where they had started running, we found a Japanese soldier lying along the stream, groaning. We realized he had been shot in the upper thigh. It was a nasty wound.

A young native used his machete to cut two bamboo stocks to carry the wounded soldier to the stockade. Two of us took off our fatigue jackets, buttoned them up and put the bamboo stalk through the sleeves at one end. The second person did the same at the other end. This made a stretcher to carry the wounded man to our truck, called a weapon carrier. He was lying in the back of the truck, and two of us were in the back with him. His wound was bad, and he was in pain, so he tried to get something from his pocket. I pulled his hand away, because I didn't know what he had in there. He tried several times, so I reluctantly put my hand in his pocket. I pulled out a small medicine bottle with a 4-inch-long tube wrapped around it. He wanted to suck whatever was in the small bottle. We believe it was morphine for his wound.

The soldier could not speak English, so we could not understand him. However, everybody knew what a smile meant, which was followed by him putting his hand up to his mouth and puffing. We knew what that meant, a cigarette. I didn't smoke, so one of the other soldiers gave him a cigarette. All the commotion started as we were on our way to the stockade. When we got there, I was asked to stay with the carrier, because weapons were in there. The Japanese prisoners kept watching me, and I was doing the same to them. They slept in tiers about 18 inches high and about 6 feet long, about four tiers high.

After the war was over, some of the soldiers from our unit would go over to the Marine companies to play poker after payday. There was nothing else to do, but gamble. We had a few seasoned gamblers who enjoyed the game. I didn't gamble, so they always asked me to go along in case they needed more money for gambling. I would charge them $12 for $10 or $20 for $15, and so on. The gamblers always paid their debt because they would need me again. That was my little hustle, also sewing chevrons on shirt jackets, etc. Some soldiers liked their shirts form fitting, so I would sew their shirts to show how well their bodies were sculpted. We would get tickets or cardboard coins for a drink called near beer, and I didn't keep them long. They knew I didn't drink, so this was another area for me to earn money.

Sometime in September 1945, an Associated Press photographer came to our camp selling snapshots of his travels. One of those snapshots showed the raising of the United States flag on Iwo Jima, Feb. 23, 1945. I bought a set of 71 snapshots for $3. I was not aware at the time, the photographer could have been Joe Rosenthal, who won a Pulitzer Prize and inspired the famous memorial. I first saw Joe Rosenthal on television in 2005. I typed him a letter on April 4, 2005. His daughter, Anne took care of his mail. She consulted her father concerning six or more copies of the photos I included with my letter. When he looked through those snapshots sent to him, he claimed only the image of the raising of the flag on Iwo Jima. He said the others were not taken by him. I have some reservations about that, because the flag raising could not be denied. I still have the letter of reply from his daughter. At the time of purchase I did not know it would be a prize photo.

I learned to know several Guamanian families, and one of the families invited my buddy and me to have Christmas dinner with them. We didn't like their cooking, because it was much different from our method of cooking. We tried to eat it. Part of our meal was green and wrapped in dough. My buddy and I couldn't eat it, so we threw it under the house. Most houses were built about 2 feet off the ground. Some chickens saw us throw it under the house and went after it, clucking loudly and fighting over it. They brought it out from under the house, and we were embarrassed. The family looked at the chickens eating it, and so did we. We said after we left their home that we are not going to be invited there again. We laughed practically all the way back to the camp.

Brothers Voni, 7, and McKinley, Jr., 5,
dressed for Sunday school.

Voni Grimes' graduation photograph, class of 19m42,
William Penn High School.

Voni Grimes, U.S. Army Air Force, June 1944.

Voni, 22, on Saipan. Today, Grimes still carries those six packs, working out three times a week "and then some" at the York gym that bears his name and at Crispus Attucks Community Center.

Irene Grimes, Voni's first wife, seen in June 1946. Voni and Irene were married for 24 years when Irene died of cancer.

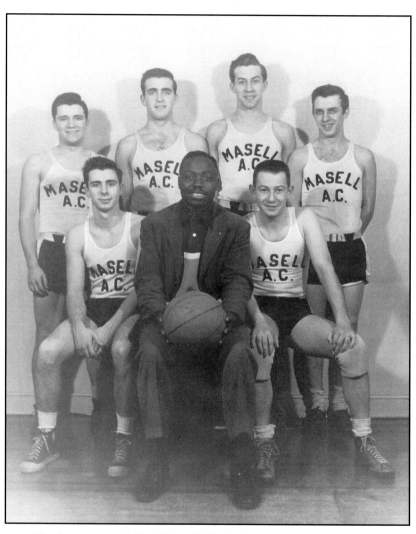

Voni managed the Masell (Cole Steel) basketball team in the 1950s and 1960s.

Voni is pictured with beloved community leader Helen Thackston at a Crispus Attucks awards ceremony. CA then was located in a converted East Maple Street church.

Voni and Lorrayne Grimes' four daughters and son: first row, from left, Johnsie Silas and Edgar (Pete) Gibson. Second row, from left, Beverly DeVan, Toni Thompson and Neomi Davis.

*York County Parks Board member Voni Grimes meets
Richard M. Nixon, during the former president's visit
to his namesake park in the late 1980s.*

*Two shodan recognize Voni for his years of
instruction in the martial arts.*

Voni is surrounded by administrators on his retirement from Penn State York: From left, John Marshall, director of continuing education; John J. Romano, CEO, Penn State York; Ed Elias, Romano's predecessor as CEO; and Frank Miller, campus registrar.

Voni meets Jerry Falwell aboard the evangelist's plane at York Airport in the 1980s. Voni was then serving as a member of the Foreman's Club (Industrial Management Club), and Falwell served as a guest speaker at a club event. Voni had offered to take Falwell to dinner, and Falwell, needing to return to Virgina, chose fare from a Burger King drive-through. The pair ate on the plane.

Voni as grand inspector general of the 33rd and last degree of Scottish Rite Masonry, 1986.

Voni stands outside his Florida vacation home at Silver Springs Shore.

Voni's brother-in-law, the Rev. Irvin Kittrell,
is pictured with his wife and Voni's sister, Margaret.

Voni in his home, 112 Lynbrook Drive South, in 1993.
He lived in that Springettsbury Township neighborhood
before fulfilling his dream of living in the Yorktowne Hotel.

Personal Care Home

*Voni, Lorrayne and a twinned district governor and first lady
from Sydney, Australia at the Lions International
convention in Hawaii in June 2000.*

Voni stands on the Great Wall of China during his visit there for a Lions International Convention in 2005.

Voni received this memento for his visit to the Great Wall.

Ron Martin emcees a World Lions Service Week observance
on Oct. 1, 2000, in York's Continental Square during
Voni's year as Lions 14-C district governor.

Voni delights York Revolution fans by playing
'The Star Spangled Banner' on his harmonica, August, 2007.

DISTRICT GOVERNOR'S MESSAGE

TO: LIONS, LIONESS AND LEOS

I greet you in the name of our Lord Jesus Christ, love and friendship as we chart our path into the future.

THE TIME IS NOW:
⇒ for us to make a "BREAKTHROUGH" into the new millennium.
THE TIME IS NOW:
⇒ for growth and awareness.
THE TIME IS NOW:
⇒ for all Lions and Lioness to be an Evangelist for Lionism.
THE TIME IS NOW:
⇒ to be a participator, not a spectator.
THE TIME IS NOW:
⇒ for innovative thinking and new ideas. Where there is no vision, men perish.

We are sounding a call for service and self-empowerment. Each Lion and Lioness must take upon him/herself to continue to give of themselves service to others. Together we must continue to identify the needs of community and join hands, hearts and minds to make it better for those "WE SERVE."

It is an opportunity for all Lions and Lioness to recall the fundamental reason for our existence. It also shows our community that our clubs are really involved in the community.

I leave you with this thought: We are not going to move from where we are on the basis of who we are.

Yours in Lionism,

Voni B. Grimes
Governor
District 14-C

LOVE
LIFE
LABOR
LOYALTY
LIBERTY
LAW
LION

As Governor, I have a charge to keep — to recognize certain needs of our fellow Lions, which are as follows:

1) **Emotional security:**
We want to create a climate of "trust" and make fellow Lions and Lioness feel that their contributions are worthwhile and aimed at our goals.

2) **Self-expression:**
One should not feel he or she has to surrender his or her heritage when attending meetings. You have the right to communicate ideas and suggestions, etc., without fear or retribution.

3) **Recognition:**
We must continue to give recognition, when in order.

4) **Self-respect:**
This must be earned.

**NOT ABOVE YOU,
NOT BELOW YOU,
BUT WITH YOU.**

The Lions International District Governor for York, Adams and Cumberland counties has his say in this 14-C directory, 2000-2001.

Voni B. Grimes, at the Yorktowne Hotel.
(York Daily Record/Sunday News photo)

Voni B. Grimes, in 2008.

Chapter 5

Post-war years:
Getting started

In March 1946, we traveled by ship to Saipan. While there, we didn't do much but wait until it was time to go back to the states. The date of departure for home on the S.S. Cape Clear was April 8, 1946, and we arrived on April 22, 1946. I was honorably discharged from the 246th Ordnance Ammunition Company at Fort Dix Separation Center, Fort Dix, N.J., on May 1, 1946. The same day, I went to the bus station to get a bus to York, Pa. When I arrived at the York bus station, my wife and the entire family were there to welcome me home. That was a great day that I will always remember.

Irene and I lived at 112 S. Newberry Street with my mother. She was still working as a keypunch operator. Within two weeks after being discharged, I was hired by Jones and Sipe Body Repair Company. I fixed dented fenders and did other work, using my sheet metal skills. Later, I worked for York Hoover, making bodies and parts for trucks.

I wanted to purchase a car as my buddies were doing. My wife asked, "Hon (as she called me since we started dating), why should we buy a car when we don't have a house of our own."

We prayed about where we wanted to be when we were 50 years old - and 75 years old. We were only 24 at that time. We prayed to God to help us plan our entire lives. We knew planning meant nothing if we didn't execute it. We would work very hard to reach our goal. We agreed that we would buy real estate until we were 50 years old. And we did. We accumulated 12 properties - apartments and single houses.

At that time, one could purchase a house for $3,000 to $4,000. At the time, that amount could purchase quality houses. The most I ever paid for a property was $6,500 and the other was $8,000. We managed to buy these properties by making a deal with the loan officer at the bank that we were using. He would call me: "Voni, I have a property on East Philadelphia Street. Check it out. If you like it, let's talk about it." If I liked it, I would offer him a down payment, or he would tell me how much he needed for a down payment. Sometimes, we would agree, and sometimes we would not. When the loan officer attended his weekly or bi-weekly meetings, he did not have to say, "I had to foreclose on John Doe's mortgage. Voni Grimes purchased the property." I had a Realtor handle our properties, because it was the best thing to do.

We agreed that when we arrived at 50 years of age, we would move into our dream house. Our dream house would be an upscale house – the type that then was not available to colored people. That was very unfair, because some of us could have afforded an up-scale house. That's why I bought a Cadillac, because they couldn't stop me from purchasing the best car on the market.

When we were 75 years old, we agreed we would move into the Yorktowne Hotel, because during the 1940s colored people were not welcomed. When famous colored entertainers, such as Cab Calloway, played at the Valencia Ballroom, they were not welcomed to stay at the Yorktowne Hotel. They had to stay in the homes of colored residents. Helen Peaco and her husband usually had a standing invitation for colored entertainers. The colored people who were hired did menial jobs such as operating the elevator, carrying luggage and waiting tables.

Between the ages of 24 to 45, we had no children of our own, but we had a deep love for our nieces and nephews, especially Tony (Anthony) Grimes and Reggie Ellis. They had no father in the home. Both were academically solid. Tony graduated from a computer school and was inducted shortly after that into the Vietnam War, and Reggie went to college. After the war and college, they both had good jobs, and they got married to two lovely ladies, Juanita and Judy, respectively. Tony had two boys who were academically solid and college graduates, one a West Point graduate. One is an attorney and the other is a chef at the Yorktowne Hotel. Tony has since passed away. Reggie has three boys: one in college, one a drummer and the other a computer wiz. Reggie once told me: "Uncle Bus (as he calls me), you have taught me well. I have planned my life also. I have real estate and other things that I'm doing." Reggie is aware that real estate increases in value, and cars decrease in value.

God blessed us to have a wonderful life together. We belonged to Small Memorial A. M. E. Zion Church. Irene and I traveled abroad every year, sometimes twice a year. My wife had a convertible, an Austin Healy Sprite, and her standard white French poodle, which she enjoyed very much. She would sometimes tint the poodle the color of the dress she was wearing. We bought the poodle directly from France in the early 1950s. We picked him up at the Philadelphia Airport. All of his pedigree documents were typed in French. We trained Frenchy (Pierre, the French Painter) at the Shipley Estates, East Market Street, near Hallam. He was in dog shows around Pennsylvania, particularly the Convention Hall in Philadelphia. We belonged to the A. K. C., American Kennel Club, which met once a month in Lancaster. We would have our meeting in a large room, and the dogs would have their meeting in the back room wearing little Halloween hats, with a person assigned to watch and play with them. When we went to those meetings, the dogs were always glad to see that person.

My experience of wanting to purchase a house first on Elm Street in York and then in the 1950s on Haines Road was out of the question, because a Realtor refused to show properties there to me. Nevertheless, he took me out to a remote, weedy area between Hallam and Wrightsville and told me a man he knew would be willing to sell the land to me.

I moved to 330 E. Locust St. in York and purchased a Cadillac. The Realtor stopped me from wanting to live where I wanted, but the Realtor could not stop me from buying a Cadillac. Again, that is why I drive a Cadillac to this day. My Cadillac will always remind me of why I purchased it.

Irene died of cancer in 1968. I took her to the doctor for an unidentified lump on her breast. The doctor advised us to go directly to the York Hospital to get more information. After going to the hospital and undergoing many tests, the doctor told her that she had cancer, and she would have to be admitted. He told her that it was terminal.

My wife asked the doctor, "How long do I have to live? I can take it."

He told her about three and a half months. She immediately turned to me and asked, "Will you promise me that you will get a complete physical every year?"

I said, "I promise."

I have been receiving physicals for 40 years and still counting. It pays to obey, because I don't take any medication at all, not even an aspirin. However, I'm not stupid. If it's life threatening I will follow my doctor's order.

Irene never had a chance to move into our dream house that we had worked very hard for. I prayed to God to give me another good wife. Good on the inside as well as on the outside. He gave me a wife not only good on the inside and outside, but also beautiful.

Chapter 6

My wife,
Lorrayne

In the latter part of 1968, a former renter of one of my apartments, who had moved to Harrisburg because of her employment at the State Capitol, called me and asked if I was ready for dating. This lady, she said, doesn't have a husband, and she is your type. I told her no. Later, she asked again, and I gingerly agreed.

"I am going to invite you up here for dinner, and I want you to meet this wonderful lady; just your type and she is a Christian," she said.

I said to myself, "God answers prayers."

Our first meeting was very good. Our next meeting was to meet her family. I felt very comfortable. She had five children: four girls and one boy. Four of her children were grown and on their own and doing well. The fifth child, Toni, was 14 years old and in junior high school at that time. The names of the other four are Johnsie and Pete (who makes you laugh), Naomi (very serious and quiet) and Beverly (a professional singer). B. B. King had encouraged her as she opened at the Apollo in New York City. She died on June 24, 2007.

I married Lorrayne on March 31, 1969. Let me tell you about Lorrayne, who has now been my wife for 39 years. She is beautiful on the inside as well as the outside. Everything that I have done for the amelioration of our community or organizations, she has supported me 100 percent. Otherwise, I could not have attained the things that were and are attainable for my family and me. Involving one's self in the community and organizations take time and funds, and she is always there for me. She is a great part of my life. We traveled extensively, out of the country as well as in our country. We enjoy our time-shares in Nassau, Bahamas, and Atlantic City, N. J.

One cannot say with justification, "When I get more time, I'm going to do these things." There are only 24 hours in a day. There is not going to be more time in a day, so we have to prioritize our time and decide what is important and what is eminent to us. Then make your choice. Manage your funds while you are young; operate on a budget. When you are retired, you and your spouse can enjoy the fruits of your labor. Sometimes, we say absurd things like, "I don't know if I'm going to live that long." If you do, you can live happy the rest of your life. Happiness is for you. We are only custodians of what we accomplished on this Earth.

We brought nothing into this world, and we will take nothing out. One fellow said, "I don't know how much I will have to pay on the way." Shortly thereafter, this gentleman passed away. At his viewing, he had $100,000 lined up in his casket. Three of his buddies noticed the cash in his casket. One of the buddies took his checkbook out of his pocket and wrote him a check for $100,000, then asked the other two buddies to help him put the money in his bag. When that chore was completed, he put the check in the casket and said, "Wherever he is going, let him cash it when he gets there."

I am a Christian. However, I have respect for everyone's religion. Some people do not believe in the Trinity, but I believe in it 100 percent. As a layman, this is the way I understand it: Let's take a married man who has a complete family, and some member doesn't believe in the Trinity – the Father, Son and Holy Spirit. How can three men be one? Let's take John Doe. He is a husband, but who are we talking about? John Doe. He is a son, but who are we talking about? John Doe. He is a brother, but who are we talking about? John Doe. If John Doe can be one person acting in three or more different categories and addressing each differently, why can't God act in three different categories or as many as he wants to? There is one difference, and that is: "He is holy." This may not be proper from a theological standpoint, but my analogy of the Trinity is the way I can understand it.

But back to Lorrayne: My wife has never been a spectator; she has always been a participator. For example, in 1970, she was involved in the youth division of the York Recreation Commission, teaching poise and etiquette for girls between the ages of 10 through 18. She also produced a pageant called, "Miss Fine Brown Frame" for eight years. She served as vice president of Yorktowne A. B. W. (American Business Women Association.) She retired from Children and Youth Services, placement unit.

In 1987, she became the grand worthy matron, Order of Eastern Star, P.H.A., state of Pennsylvania. Speaking in Wilkes-Barre, she received the key to the city. She received many citations: Senate of Pennsylvania, House of Representatives; Legion of Honor Award, Chapel of Four Chaplains; and other honors throughout Pennsylvania and beyond.

Lorrayne and I have traveled extensively. The most thrilling was when she and my mother traveled to the Holy Land: the catacombs, the Wailing Wall, the Jordan River and other places of interest. She also brought back water from the Jordan River.

One of Lorrayne's honors came from Vice President George and Barbara Bush for her years of tireless and selfless service on behalf of others - and me.

Chapter 7

Education pays off

I was employed at Cole Steel Equipment Company prior to seeking a position at Penn State University, York Campus, as business manager. I was a career student at the time, having 23 years of schooling, counting senior high school. I never received a post-secondary degree but took a variety of courses: three years of mechanical engineering, one year and a half of accounting, philosophy, and psychology, abnormal psychology, a course of phrenology (pseudo psychology), two years of Spanish and three years of Russian languages.

As a black man, I thought it was almost impossible to get a job of the magnitude of that Penn State position. However, it is better to have an education and not need it than to need an education and not have it. I said to myself, "I will not get the position because of my color." Never second-guess anyone, because you really don't know. I was surprised when I went into the office of Mr. Ed Elias, C.E.O., Penn State York, for an interview, and he asked, "What do you have to offer?" I told him I had three years of mechanical engineering and all my other completed courses. After looking at my blueprints and accounting ability, he said, "Voni, I'm going to hire you. I know how hard it was to get where I am, because I'm Lebanese. We are a young campus, and we can use your skills."

My first assignment was to work with the architect for the completion of the gymnasium and the library, which was just about finished. The York campus was boxed in, so I purchased houses on the west side of Albemarle Street as they became available; I had a budget to purchase them. On the east side of Albemarle Street where the tiered parking lot is located today, I purchased land where a flower shop was located at the top and turned it into a parking lot. Our tennis courts, the student building and main classroom building were built during my administration. As another example of my duties, I took four days off at the end of one school year to go to the company that makes tablet-arm chairs in Missouri to purchase 1,000 units. These units would be used in the next academic year when the building would be completed for the start of school. I asked the architect to contact the general contractor to complete the largest room, the auditorium, to store the tablet-arm chairs, so they would be there for the start of school.

During my administration, the York campus was the first branch to have a keypunch maintenance program. Computers were not available at that time. When they were available, we updated our maintenance program using computers. Directors of business services at all 17 branch campuses would meet at University Park with the vice president for business once a month for a couple of days to share what we were doing at each campus. The vice president asked me to share my computer program technique with the other directors, so they might use the same technique at their campuses. My duties covered the buildings, grounds, maintenance, budgeting for the bookstore, campus utilities and maintenance department. That meant hiring for my area of operation and anything else our C.E.O. would have me do. I loved the position, because it was challenging.

My office housed my secretary and the person who handled purchasing. Across the hall was the bookstore. I had a very competent manager running the store. We sold books, jewelry, Penn State ties, T-shirts, jackets, calculators, slide-rules and other items. Whatever you needed for class, we sold it. We also had buy-back book sales.

I was asked, because I had a black belt in Judo, to teach it as a one-credit course, but my schedule was too full. So I taught it for 14 years as an extracurricular activity course, 6 to 8 p.m. I had full classes of men and women who really enjoyed it, because Judo taught discipline and how to protect oneself. It was especially good for women, because it taught them what to do and what not to do in certain situations.

Chapter 8

Memorable moments

In my early days I grew up with friends, and I still call them my friends.

To name a few: Archie Green, Harold (Jiggs) Parker, Earnie Calhoun, William Myers, Rubin Green, Beverly (Bebb) Boanes, James (Jimmie) Harley, Henry (Hab) Kirkland, Brice Jackson, Emery (Ducky) Dorm, Gregg Generette, Bob Ellicker, Edgar Kreiger, Sr., and many more. We had good times together. We were very close. At that time, we prided ourselves in attending church and having respect for others, more especially having respect for our parents, our church family, our teachers and the police. We knew the police who walked our streets or alley by name.

Some of the things we did were play pick-up hardball and softball. We also played midget softball as a team and played in other city parks. Some of us had our own bicycles, and those who did not rented from Red Kleindeinst for 15 cents an hour - and 25 cents an hour for the balloon tire bicycles (Road Masters). After school we headed for Crispus Attucks for our club meetings or to play games and table tennis.

At Hannah Penn and William Penn, we met more friends: John Zimmerman, Robert Becker, George Barkley, Ernie Horn, Gregg Woolridge and a few others. After school we played softball or basketball just to get away from studying all day in school. All of these men are now successful, but they did not forget their friends.

We frequented just a few places at that time. Those who were old enough went to Brotherly Love Elks Lodge #228, Smittie's Bar and Charles E. Williams American Legion Post #794. I didn't drink, but I enjoyed dancing. And sometimes these establishments would have entertainment that I also enjoyed.

My Masonic friends were many: John Murdaugh ('Hi Bo'), Raymond Crenshaw, Herman Hawkins, George Ruffin, Gordon (Gordy) Williams, Leon Wilson, Leroy Atwater, James Edmonds and many more.

* * *

My music remains important. When I was 4 or 5 years old, my parents bought me a mouth organ, as they were called then. Now they are called harmonicas. Well, at that time I was just a blower, in and out. In the Bible, it is written, one does not have to be in tune, just make a joyful noise. My mother would say, "Voni, stop making that noise" – it must not have been joyful at all. When I was about 10 or 12 years old, I purchased a mouth organ to learn how to play it. My first song was "Silent Night," but it wasn't Christmas time. For some reason, I just abruptly stopped. I did not try to play it again until I was in my 60s.

I am a Mason, and I used to sing in our Grand Lodge Choir in Philadelphia. In our choir, one brother played the harmonica. It sounded very good, so I said to myself, "I can do that." You can do many things, but you must believe in yourself. I told my wife about the brother in the choir blowing the harmonica. I said to her, "I am going to buy a harmonica and learn how to play it." The following week, she purchased one for me. That was the motivator to get me started. Now I feel very comfortable playing alone or for someone else. I do not play by music. You hum it, and I will play it.

* * *

Shortly after Lorrayne and I were married in 1969, we moved to 112 Lynbrook Drive South, Springettsbury Township - a high-end neighborhood. Within a month, the neighbors of Lynbrook Drive invited Lorrayne to a brunch to welcome her to the community. The pastor from the church nearby invited us to worship with them. We were well received as their neighbor.

We also had our granddaughter, Amber, living with us. She was going to a private school in Harrisburg, but we told our daughter, Johnsie, that Amber could come to York and get the same quality of education at a school in Springettsbury. She graduated and went to college. She is now a registered nurse at a hospital in Philadelphia. She is married and has a 6-year-old son. Our other granddaughter, Wendy DeVan, came to live with us for a shorter period, and she is also a college graduate. She has a very good position with an insurance company in the Philadelphia area.

One day I was mowing my front lawn, and a landscaper pulled up along the curb and said, "I am looking for Voni Grimes."

I said, "I'm Voni Grimes."

He smiled, as if to say "yeah."

"I am supposed to do some landscaping in his backyard - put in some plants, flowers etc," he said.

Another such incident came in 1973, when we received a letter between the storm door and the door - not in our mailbox. This letter was from the "United Klans of America Inc., Knights of the Ku Klux Klan."

There were five pages plus a Swastika, and all pages degraded black people in the most horrible way. The writer was a terrorist. They were asking us to join, thinking we were white. They had no idea we were the only black family in the community. My wife saved everything that was in the envelope. We still have it today. He was from York Haven. I will not give his name, address or telephone number. It was an "Application for Citizenship in the Invisible Empire" and provided an address for return mail.

***

We lived at Lynbrook Drive for 30 good years, and then we moved into the Yorktowne Hotel, living there for another five good years. We were like family while living there. My picture had hung among other pictures in the Yorktowne's Autographs Restaurant for a couple of years before we moved in to the hotel.

We now reside in Green Springs, because of the amenities for our grandchildren. They use the tennis courts, swings, animated animal rides and swimming pool. We had two splash parties for the kids since we have been here.

Our prayers to own our dream house by age 50 and to live the Yorktowne Hotel at age 75 were fulfilled.

We are living life abundantly.

I hope you enjoyed my memoir. This is my life as I've lived it.

Appendix I

Community activities

- I became a trustee in our church (Small Memorial A.M. E. Zion) in 1948 and served for many years. I became an honorary trustee in 1961, by the Rev. Baker. Now after serving many more years, I am an emeritus trustee and still attending meetings when I can.

- I was superintendent of Small's Sunday School, 1950 through 1970 - a beautiful plaque was presented to me for my services of those years.

- I am a founding member of York County Legal Service, and as the service began to spread over other counties, we called it Central Pennsylvania Legal Services. It started doing business in an office near the southeast corner of South Queen and East King streets. At that time I was employed at Cole Steel, and with our funding for office equipment, I purchased all that was needed for that location (a partly renovated row house). We started with two people, a secretary and another person to handle the incoming information to be passed on to the attorney. As the workload became heavier, other attorneys were made available including a Hispanic attorney. During that time, it became necessary, because of an influx of Spanish-speaking people moving to the York area for a better life.

- I am co-founder of the York County Parks and Recreation Department. It was born at the Pine Street School Building, corner of Pine and Philadelphia streets. I was the director of the Princess Street Recreation Center. Joseph Raab, president of the York County Commissioners, and I were attending a Girls Club party. Joe, as he was called, said, "Voni, you know, we do not have any county recreation for our youth and adults. We need to do something." While munching on cookies and drinking punch, we walked outside to sit on the picnic benches to discuss it further. He said, "Come to my chamber at the Courthouse and we will see what can be done." We discussed county parks in detail, then we picked five people from our community "Citizen's Study Committee 1968." This committee was to select a board of directors. Those selected were the first board members of the "York County Board of Parks and Recreation": Harry McLaughlin, chairman; the Rev. Carroll C. Luckenbaugh, vice chairman; Sylvia Newcombe, secretary; Voni B. Grimes, treasurer; J. Kerr Anderson; Carroll T. Hunt; P. Joseph Raab; John R. Rinehart; Ray R. Wiegand.

- I am a founding member of Access. I was the person who cleaned out the entire basement of the Access building, so that we could move in. We had meetings at the United Way, East King Street. I taught the first president of Access, Judo. Access has grown to become a wonderful program, helping battered women.

- I am a founding member of C.P.C. (Community Progress Council), located in the 200 block of East College Avenue. Also serving was Atty. Harry Rubin, President, and about five others: Prof. Joseph Douglas; Robert Erdos; State Senator Harry Seyler; Edith Barber. If I missed anyone, please forgive me, because it has been a long time.

- I was the first director of the Princess Center. We had many programs working with children. Some of the highlights of our programs were taking the children to farms to see how vegetables grow. This was the first time for many of our children. This is not a joke. An 8-year-old student asked the farmer, our guide, "What are those plants?" "Egg plants," he was told. He rushed back to his older brother and said, "This guy grows his own eggs." We take everything for granted, but a child doesn't know, because his experience is limited. We took three busloads of children to the zoo in Baltimore and that afternoon to Washington, D.C., to the Smithsonian Institution. The children enjoyed the entire day but were tired when they arrived home. These children are grown up now, and they are good parents, grandparents, doctors, lawyers and PhDs. One of the future PhDs was my secretary, when she was a very bright student attending the Princess Center. I don't want to name names, because I loved all of them. I was also president of the York Recreation Commission, 1973.

- I was chairman of York County Vocational Technical School Advisory Committee - now known as York County School of Technology Adult and Continuing Education Center - for three years, 1986-1988. Because of its growth in students, the school is a mega-sized building. The highlight of my tenure was engaging one of our members, David Carver, to produce a video of the programs. He did an excellent job.

- I was a member on the Advisory Board of the AAA of Southern Pennsylvania for 28 years. Of those years, I served from 1984 to 1996 as secretary. There are eight branches doing an excellent job.

- I was a member of the York County Chamber of Commerce and also chaired a committee. I joined the chamber of commerce when my wife and I purchased a personal care business. We had 20 men and women whom we loved very much. That was our family, and we all felt very comfortable together. Every month we had a program for them, designed by Helen Gotwalt, a retired teacher at William Penn Senior High School. The staff would conduct a program Christmas morning. The residents all came downstairs early to see what Santa had brought them.We had our personal care home for 12 years. We miss our family: Some are deceased while others have gone back to their families or to nursing homes. In 2005, I received the chamber's community service award.

- I was given the Key to the City, First Capital of the U.S., York, Pennsylvania. At that time, I was District Governor, 14-C, The International Association of Lion Clubs, covering 3,000 members. As governor, I had a 25-foot banner made by Imagineered Signs and Displays, Inc., placed over Continental Square saying, "WORLD LIONS SERVICE WEEK". I still have that banner. The city provided its public address system for the event that took place in the square on Oct. 1, 2000. Ron Martin, anchorman for WGAL, was our master of ceremonies. There were past district governors who were on the program. Each explained a segment of Lionism, and likewise, the C.E.O. of the Blind Center explained how the Lion Clubs have helped the blind financially and otherwise. Just before the program was adjourned, Lorrayne and I gave Ron a multicolored glass Lion that we had purchased in Hawaii. At the end of the program, our balloon team released more than 300 balloons, as I played "God Bless America" on my harmonica. A video was made of the program, which I still have. Several proclamations were given for the event by the Honorable Charles H. Robertson, mayor of the City of York; County Commissioners Christopher B. Reilly and Shirley L. Glass, and Charles R. Noll, county administrator; and State Representative Stephen H. Stetler.

- I was a grand marshal of the Halloween Parade, 1988. During the parade, the convertible in which I was riding stopped in front of the courthouse and the Honorable Mayor William

76

Althaus, City of York, gave me a pewter plate that I still cherish very much.

- I received my black belt in Judo in 1960. I was active in the martial arts for 28 years. I received a black belt certification to the rank of soke shihan. I was honored in 1996 at Crispus Attucks Community Center. We had a light repast with members of the Baltimore, Harrisburg and York City dojos. I taught martial arts at the Princess Center and Penn State York Campus for 14 years. I was asked to teach it as a one-credit course, but I became too busy doing my regular job as director of business services. However, I taught it after school hours, a couple of nights a week.

- I received the 33rd Degree in Masonry, 1986, and I am still a member of The Grand Orient, Philadelphia. I am a member of The United Supreme Council, of the Sovereign Grand Inspector General of the 33rd and Last Degree of the Ancient and Accepted Scottish Rite of Free Masons (Prince Hall Affiliation) for the Northern Jurisdiction of the United States of America.

- After York Junior College moved to its present location, the gymnasium was called the "College Avenue Gym." On Oct. 30, 1984, it was renamed the "Voni B. Grimes Gymnasium" by Mayor Wiliam J. Althaus and York City Council. Mayor Althaus also proclaimed that day as "Voni B. Grimes Day." The gymnasium has many programs - basketball, soccer, volleyball (county leagues and special semi- pro teams appear at times), a fitness center (I am a member). The Christmas program for children is our main attraction, because we give Christmas toys to the children in the community. Some parents depend on those toys for their children's Christmas.

- Cyber Center, 2101 Pennsylvania Ave., York: Charles H. Falkler was founder and chairman of the first Management Group

Committee, and I was among the first members selected. Charles was honored for his achievements, and a plaque is placed outside the door where our meetings were held.

- In 1984, I was invited by Dale Peters, a Realtor and a very fine neighbor, to join the International Association of Lions Clubs, District 14-C. Realizing it is a service organization, I joined after attending one meeting. I eventually became a district governor, 2000 to 2001. I was officially installed in Hawaii, because the governors (741 from 196 countries) elected that year were there to learn more and to be sworn in. We were there five days before the International Convention started. Through that experience, Lorrayne and I had an opportunity to meet Lions from many countries. In 2005, the International Lions Convention was in China, and I was able to attend. I was there for three weeks. The 14 hours I was in the air from San Francisco to Beijing, China, meant that I needed to be there for three weeks. The one-week convention was in Hong Kong, and I took a two-week vacation while there.

- I organized a new Lions Club in 1984, called South York Lions Club. I received a plaque from Lions Club International for that effort.

- I received the 23rd edition of "Who's Who in Finance and Industry," which included my name, in 1983, and a plaque for gaining that honor. Also, the seventh edition of "Who's Who among Black Americans," which included my name, in 1993, and a certificate. Also, the Platinum Edition of "Who's Who Worldwide," which included my name, in 1993, and a plaque.

- Other accolades, with proclamations:

  - World Lions Service Week, October, 1 - 8, 2000, the Board of County Commissioners, Christopher B. Reilly, president.

  - World Lions Service Week, October, 1 - 8, 2000, Commonwealth of Pennsylvania, House of Representatives, Stephen Stetler, sponsor, and Matthew Ryan, speaker of the House.

  - The Governor's "Silver and Gold" award, Senate of Pennsylvania, Oct., 2, 2001, Gov. Mark S. Schweiker and Sen. Michael Waugh. For loyal and dedicated commitment to enhance the quality of life for older Pennsylvanians.

  - Black History, Feb. 26, 2006, honored by Deborah Chapter, #26, Order of the Eastern Star, Prince Hall Affiliated. Received a proclamation from the Board of County Commissioners, Lori O. Mittrick, president, for outstanding leadership in our community, philanthropic endeavors, positive efforts for the youth in our community and many lives touched through desire to build a better world through the knowledge of our rich and diverse heritage. At the same event, I received a proclamation from Mayor John S. Brenner, citing: my awareness that mentoring and nurturing children is vital to a community's future and my involvement with Logos Academy, where I helped young people of the community value the importance of an education. Sunday, Feb. 26, 2006, was proclaimed as a day to pay tribute to "Voni B. Grimes, one of York's most worthy citizens."

Appendix II

Trip to China, 2005

Starting on June 13, 2005, nine Lions and district governors - I being one of the district governors - enjoyed a 14-hour trip from San Francisco to Beijing, crossing the International Date Line. We were in China for three weeks: two weeks vacationing and the third week as a part of the 88th Lions Club International Convention, June 27, to July 1, 2005, in Hong Kong. Our clubs are located worldwide in 200 countries, with 1.3 million members in over 43,000 clubs. Every other year, the Lions Club International Convention is held in a different country. Using those times to take your vacation, you become a World Traveler.

My two weeks' vacation before being a part of the International Convention on the third week was awesome. We checked into the 5 Star Prime Hotel with spacious rooms. You are given a plastic card for entering your room. After entering, you place your plastic card in a holder on the wall inside the door, and the lights come on. Leaving your room, you remove the plastic card from the holder on the wall and the lights go out, saving electricity. While in China, we visited many worthwhile places. To name a few: Beijing Zoo, Beihai Park, Chairman Mao Memorial Hall. Tiananmen Square, the largest public square in the world. The Great Wall of China is of formidable construction that winds its way over hills for more than 2,000 miles. We visited the Badaling section of the Wall. It is noted for its panoramic views. In this area, I climbed 888 steps in about 2 ½ hours. I have a plaque that says; "This certifies that Voni Grimes did climb the Great Wall of China June 16, 2005." We visited the Ming Tombs, burial site of the Ming Dynasty. The next day, we flew from Beijing to Xian. We had a Tai Chi demonstration at the 15th Century Temple of Heaven. I also enjoyed the jinrikisha tour of the Hutong area.

Xian is most famous for the tomb of China's first emperor, guarded by thousands of terra-cotta warriors. Peasant farmers digging a well first discovered the head of a terra-cotta warrior in 1974. We spent the afternoon at the excavation site that started that year. I have an autographed copy of the book; "Qin's Terra-Cotta Army." By the way, they are life-size warriors and horses as well. Before our flight to Chongqing, we visited the Han Yangling Museum. In Xian, we attended the Shaanxi Grand Opera House. We had dinner, followed by the opera. Their costumes were beautiful, but the performance was in Chinese. It was a very good evening. My first opera was in the Chinese language.

We landed in Chongqing to take a four-day cruise on the deluxe Viking Sky ship on the Yangtze River. When we boarded the ship, the river was somewhat muddy. We were told it is called the "Golden Yangtze." During our cruise, the guide would share many stories and legends with us. By the way, the farther we cruised, the brighter the Yangtze became.

For the next 150 miles, the Yangtze was very clear, and the ship forced its way through a spectacular barrier of solid limestone ridges know as the Three Gorges - Qutang, Wushan and Wu Gorges.

The Three Gorges Dam is 1.3 miles wide and 610 feet tall. The dam is China's largest construction project since the Great Wall. Never before has a dam of this magnitude been attempted. (By the way, I am copying this information from what was given to us.) China decided to dam the Yangtze in 1994 with a wall of steel and concrete that would take 15 years and over $30 billion to build. When completed, the dam will contain twice the amount of concrete of the Itaipu Dam in Brazil, the world's largest. It will create a 5 trillion-gallon reservoir hundreds of feet deep and about 385 miles long. The dam is said to be built to withstand an earthquake measuring 7.0 on the Richter Scale. It will transform the Yangtze River into a more navigable waterway and protect the middle and lower reaches of the river from disastrous floods. The dam's hydroelectric turbines are expected to create the equivalent electricity of 18 nuclear power plants.

The dam is located near the mouth of the lowest of the Three Gorges, where the current is divided by an island. In November 1997, the first stage was completed with the blocking of two-thirds of the river's width. The water level had risen 59 feet by the end of 1998, and it had gone up an additional 171 feet by November 2003. Ninety-eight feet will be added by 2009, with an additional 33 feet that year, when the dam will come into full operation. Smaller ships will use a single-stage lift and larger ones five stepped locks. The waters in the Three Gorges will rise a total of 361 feet, gradually changing the scenery in the area. We learned what the dam means to the Chinese people and how the country has dealt with the displacement of more than 1 million people and submergence of more than 1,000 cities and villages. That evening, we flew to Hong Kong.

Hong King is the hub of Asia. We transferred to our hotel, Marco Polo Hong Kong Hotel in Harbour City, Kowloon. We enjoyed free time upon arrival. The next morning, we boarded the tram for a ride to the top of Victoria Peak. From that vantage point, we had a panoramic view of the modern high-rise buildings and other points of interest. That afternoon we were free to explore the city on our own. Hong Kong reminds me of New York City, with its beautiful skyscrapers, multitudes of shops (where a suit can be made in 24 hours of very good material at an affordable price) and diversity of people. Hong Kong seems to be a friendly place. We ventured out on the Star Ferry that runs between Hong Kong Island and Kowloon to see the excellent restaurants from around the world. Something for everyone. I saw a McDonald's there also.

We enjoyed the festivities of the Lions convention. There were meetings to attend, among other things of interest, and I attended the parade that showcased the many nations in their national regalia. The trip to China was a trip I will never forget. Our guide was a female Chinese college student and really knowledgeable.

After eating breakfast, I said goodbye to China as we boarded our flight back to the U.S.A.

Education: Something I feel very strongly about

Education is a field of knowledge, dealing with technical aspects of teaching. Do you want it? Reach out and grab it.

I want to talk to you about a "Bridging Troubled Waters." I don't know you or your character; therefore, I am speaking in generalities. Speaking at you, you are not empathetic in regard to what I say. Speaking to you, I would expect you to listen and focus on what I'm saying to you. When I say something that touches a nerve, do not say, "Amen." Say, "Ouch."

I would be remiss if I, as the author, would not address the theme of "Bridging Troubled Waters."

"The Bridge"
Education. Your spiritual being. Understanding and love for each other, for once we find love we automatically find God, because God is love.

"Troubled Waters"
Temptation. Drug abuse. Alcoholism. Dropping out. Teenage pregnancy and all the negative things of life. Failure is not a terminal disease.

Young people, this is a wake-up call. Some of us take everything for granted. Whom do you depend on for your day-to-day education, counseling, activities and support - your teacher? Teachers are the people who make things happen. Don't sit around and watch things happen. Give your teacher your cooperation and the respect he or she deserves. Let us not forget, we must give respect in order to earn respect.

As you begin to cross this bridge over troubled waters, consider what I have mentioned before about success. You need education, your spiritual being, understanding and love, which lead to success or favorable results.

To have success, we must do certain things:
I want to introduce you to the 3 D's:
1 - Your direction.
2 - Your desire (embryo to success).
3 - Your determination. Have the determination to follow through to reach your goal in life.

Set a goal for yourself. Where do you want to be five years from now? In college? In a technical school? On welfare? On the streets? In jail? The choice is yours. Reach for the sky, but always include God first in your plan. However, it's not a plan if you don't execute it. We have lots of rhythm from our shoulders down, but how much rhythm do we have from our shoulders up?

We must grow. I'm not talking about in height, but in wisdom, grace and academic excellence. Do you know that growth in this fashion indicates an increase of mind? It's time for us to stop going through the motions. You are smart academically. You have the skills and other positive attributes. It's time we get it together. Each of us has a gift to lay upon the altar. I know you have what it takes to become a productive citizen of your community. You have demonstrated that many times to your friends and others. Those poems you have written, songs you have written, works of art that you have made for yourself and others and other positive things that have gained your interest. Follow your dream.

Let me share with you what I've heard. It is a frightening thing that is happening in our nation to our youth:

FROM A SODA TO CRACK AND COKE,
FROM A SLING SHOT TO AN AUTOMATIC WEAPON,
FROM CHICKEN POX TO AIDS,
FROM A CIGARETTE TO A MARIJUANA JOINT,
FROM A BROKEN LAMP TO A MOTHER'S BROKEN HEART,
FROM A HIGH SCHOOL DIPLOMA TO A JAIL TERM,
FROM A BABY DOLL TO TEENAGE PREGNANCY.

The time is now that our youths start new lives. Get back on track. One can tell who you are by the friends you keep. If you associate yourself with eagles, you will soar like an eagle to greater heights. But associating yourself with wolves, you will be howling like wolves.

The ruin of a community begins in the home. We face this because we ignore our spiritual and moral ways that we were taught. As we all know, this is a Lost Generation. More than half of our children are born out of wedlock, frown at education and more are going to jail than going to college. They are killing each other for almost nothing. Also, innocent children are being wounded or killed. Teachers are leaving the classrooms because they can no longer take the harassment, being cursed out or being hit. However, we have some young people who are good for our community and have gone on to college. I hope they will come back to York after graduation to help bring this city back to where it should be.

To end this segment: Don't follow anybody who is going nowhere.

On being interviewed

You who are being interviewed for employment. There are various styles of being interviewed. There is one suggestion you can use to set yourself above the other interviewees. It is very simple. First, make sure you are dressed for the job you desire before you go for an interview. Let's say you are the fourth person to be interviewed, and you are concerned about the interviewer selecting someone before you are interviewed. We're assuming you have done your homework, checking, for example, subsidiaries, distribution centers, or The Wall Street Journal.

Usually the interviewer works in an adjacent office. He doesn't see you nor does he know who you are. Ask the secretary for a half sheet of paper. Write these words, "My name is John Doe. I am your 10:30 a.m. appointment. Please do not hire anyone until you see me." The note is folded once and given to the secretary. You cannot take the note to the interviewer, but the secretary can. While he is interviewing, he will read the note from you that the secretary gave him. This note raises his interest, and from
a psychological standpoint, he is ready to conclude his interview.

When the next interviewee is asked by the secretary to go into the office to be interviewed, the interviewer is thinking it is John Doe, but it isn't. Therefore, his anxiety rises. This happens two more times before John Doe enters. Being delighted when John Doe announces his name, he said, "So you're John Doe; have a seat." John Doe unnoticeably scans the office for signs of his interviewer's interests. John Doe notices a picture on his desk of his family, so John Doe makes a comment about this beautiful family and the interviewer responds in an appreciative manner. John Doe also makes positive remarks about the other items mentioned above. Then the interviewer says to John, "Tell me about yourself." John begins to tell him about his schooling and what he has to offer this company and how he could be an asset. The interviewer asks if John is computer literate. John responds affirmatively. The interviewer asks if John ever is proficient in a certain computer software language. John should never say, "No, but I need training." Suppose the interviewer's company doesn't have a training program. What will John say then? I guess, go home without a job. The proper thing to say is, "Due to my being computer literate, let me familiarize myself with the equipment." When new equipment comes into an office, all employees must learn the equipment, so you are asking for the same opportunity.

When asked to lunch:

The C. E. O. has a reason for asking you to have lunch with him. He wants to see how well you handle yourself at the table, your table etiquette.

He, being the host, will sit first. If the boss is with a female, he will seat her first, then ask, "What would you like to have for lunch?" You ask him, "What's good?" He will probably say, "I'm having soup and sandwich." At that point, he is really telling you what he wants to spend on you, about $10. You do not have to order soup and sandwich, but if that is what you desire, order it. Do not order lobster tail. Do not ask for salt or pepper before tasting your soup. How do you know it needs salt or pepper without tasting it, first? I am thinking of your decision-making process. Do you think things over or research it before you make a decision or do you shoot from the hip? He wants to know that if he is called out of town, you could take his friend to lunch without embarrassing him or the company.